THE NOVEMBER PROPERTIUS

Also by Norm Sibum from Carcanet

In Laban's Field

NORM SIBUM

THE NOVEMBER PROPERTIUS

CARCANET

First published in 1998 by
Carcanet Press Limited
4th Floor, Conavon Court
12-16 Blackfriars Street
Manchester M3 5BQ

A CIP catalogue record for this book
is available from the British Library
ISBN 1 85754 303 3

The publisher acknowledges financial assistance
from the Arts Council of England

Set in 10pt Bembo by Bryan Williamson, Frome
Printed and bound in England by SRP Ltd, Exeter

To the memory of William Hoffer, sometime bookseller

Acknowledgements

Previous versions of some of these poems appeared in *Janus* 1 and 2, Vancouver B.C.

The author wishes gratefully to acknowledge the assistance of:
CONSEIL DES ARTS ET DES LETTRES DU QUEBEC

Contents

To a Reader

The sentiments timeless, the art skin-deep
Though the fear of death
Is its age-old source,
Verse is my vehicle,
    An all-terrain affair.

Even at dawn when you in your house
Draw on your cigarettes and with your eyes meet
The electric candles and the gold and silver spheres
Of the Christmas tree
So as to plunder the years of memory,
I will make for you – as I lie in bed
Half-asleep –
    Villains and heroes and romantic types.

I will devise for you arguments
With which to confute
The strategies and the confusions
That ambush pilgrims
At every pass and in every sack,
And we shall win one
    And we shall die, set upon.

I will preserve the mistakes, especially the prettiest
By which you and I and all the sports
Best maintain
Our precious lot of certainties, and you in your hills
Of the ancient, grey maples
And the lichened stones
Will have your command and company.
    You shall rejoice, hearing me.

You will say, 'That's rich! That's succinct.
Something in what you say rings true.'
    'It's alright,' I'll answer, endeavouring to calm you.

– Because verse is no science: either I mark off
The treacherous syllables
On the tips of my fingers
Or I let it rip.
Or, conservative, I will occupy
A comfort-zone
As the craft sits
   Beyond perfections I would bring to it.

   Will you hear me out then, a glass of something
Amber, sticky, warm
In your gouty hand, the world shrinking
   To its improvement, I expanding it back again?

   Or maybe you would prefer I come to you
And offer a more
      Personal
Treatment of my themes
And so, spare your eyes
The wear and tear of reading.
I'd pretend to a scholar's knowledge
   And leave my boots by the door.

   And maybe then you, even you will forget
Your aches and pains, and limber now
Reach down for pieces
Of the lovely split maple,
And piling them in the fireplace,
Construct a scene.
'Where were we?
Isn't it beautiful?' So you will describe
The devotional tree. And in the moonlight
The windows of
Patterned ice,
Bitter to touch,
Will entrance the eye,
   As does belief.

Caligula's Clown

Born of the unnatural union
Between the infirm and the lame,
In possession of my limbs,
Handsome enough,
I am Caligula's clown, good at the trade.
    Yet not all is well with me.

My pallor green, the sun on this cheek,
The moon affixed to the other
Playing tag, you're it!
Around the hippodrome of my face,
I amuse Caligula
    And he his perverts.

The imperial ears are huge.
The chin's missing through some oversight
As though, cold that day, fingers stiff,
Nature, making Caligula, botched
The lesser details. Still, the single-minded gem
Nested in its pouch – it's the exquisite handicraft,
    Source of imperial strategy – :

That Caligula would strip the oceans
Of all the pretty shells
If each conch were buying-power
    And the power accrue to him.

So I am standing on my head,
Sun and moon rocking on the floor,
Hideous pose delighting no one –
Not even the captain there
Pacing back and forth, hand on his sword,
Waiting for the night's password.
And five will get you ten
It'll be 'seashells' again
    And someone disinherited.

If all Romans were rolled together
Into one long noodle, a few chops!
It's done. And Caligula collects
    Enough to hire himself a decent cook for once.

    Last night, it was poets.
Caligula had it in for them
Who wouldn't hurt a fly
And between the lot couldn't squeeze
Two coins together. But their monopoly on
Rome's 'tragic destiny'
    Just about sent our master around the bend. . . .

        'Run!' he barked at me. 'Run, run, run!' –
        And he's such a stickler for the sense.

    There I was on my hands, meant to go
And fetch the man a hammer.
I did, with great dispatch.
I slapped away on the marble, while Caligula,
Rather thoughtful, lectured an innocent statue
On its overly dim outlook.
I come back. With my feet, I give over
    The tool. Caligula starts in with emphasis.

    And because I had the foresight
To put in me lots of water,
Because Caligula said, 'Do your worst,'
I released a torrent and splashed
Across the remains of Vergil's bust.
The poet had had his estate, too many
    Romans gone mad from epics.

    Did I neglect to mention
A truth to which all children are born
Who would live to ripe, old ages?
Everyone owns a fear, the disclosure of which
        embarrasses.
Discretion a good plan to follow,
Don't go telling the world

What gives you a case of nerves,
Especially if you'd avoid
    that invitation to
  A small get-together.

More than your precious privacy, ill-formed speech
Rankles Caligula. No scrambled syntax, no overblown hyperboles
  When you're screaming you're being murdered.

  Next on the list, let's see,
Yes, always the main order of business,
The thing he's always been about
Between sundown and sunup
    (when, to his disappointment,
     some ghosts prove penniless)
Is that Caligula loathes the dark
  For it might swallow him entire.

  So I distract the poor fella on slow nights
When nothing's doing, no one dribbling shit down his legs
To a pristine floor, no merchant who got lucky
Watching his luck turn.
I wriggle my extremities.
I jiggle my pisser.
I set the sun loose on the moon
  By way of my contortions.

  Some nights, Caligula says, 'There, there, my pet,
We are each a freak – it's in the blood,
But we are cunning, sir, and we will prove, one day,
That what seems unnatural is happenstance
And preserve the language.
Hurry it up! Hurry the sun's dawning.
  It has been night for too long.'

  And he will drum his fingers on his chin
If you can call the feature that.
He will wonder how he might impound
  The purse of some spice-importer.

Want to know what I hate
Besides dining off the scraps
Of his puking dinner-guests?
It's the wistful thinking I hear:
    There have been rumours.

    A spate of omens suggest that Olympian Jupiter
        was heard chuckling
From the stoop on his mountain.
A teller of fortunes claims
Caligula is not one to last,
    Time and cause unspecified.
        (Now that's prudent.)

    Then apparently, some god in a dream
Kicks Caligula with his big, right toe
And why not the left, I ask,
Or a one-two punch? Need the gods be so fussy
        when working
    Under dark's cover?

    Moon, good night.
Sun, run on your hands
Or wave your legs
    (or something to that effect),
Yes you, largest in the sky
Whom Caligula will marry come morning.
Haven't you heard?
And can you imagine what
He'll want as dowry?
    Hush! Footfalls. His.

    I'll have to be quick. Here's the scoop:
Vitellius was invited to sup, tonight.
He shows late. Was detained.
On the way, a cute thing declared his crush.
Now Vitellius has an appetite from the heavy petting.
As you know, my master is ugly.
But his smile was a piece of art.
'My dear Vitellius, how hungry?' it went.
    'Famished enough to eat a horse?'

Anyway, on my head, sun and moon rocking on the floor, I had
A great view of Vitellius's nose.
Just the barest twitch
Of his nostrils, and,
Wide open astonishment. Then the man sways a little.
    I didn't have to lick the plate.

                                    ★

    A centurion split apart Caligula's jawbone,
But Caligula, falling, cried, 'I live. I still live!'
Thirty more hacks at it
    (it was high noon)
Settled the debate,
The genitals severed,
The chin even more hopeless.
In death, as in life,
    Caligula was badly built.

    And I who was his clown
    Find my head attached, my face less green,
A hippodrome no longer,
Though I am still
Hyperventilating.
The captain will hear no more of seashells.
And Charaea stood me to my reward
        For having spurred the sun to victory.

(Suetonius wrote that Caligula feared the dark, but was expert in the art of rhetoric.)

From the Old Europa

Love was mental, lodged in the brain.
Then it worked its way loose, shrapnel piece.
Love will be as doomed as a snowflake in May
But you won't persuade anyone it's the case.
Can't fool the living. No percentage there.
Excellent noon! The girl's dress brief. The dazzling spokes
                  As bicycles pass . . .

Yes, there's the trying so hard to do right. See,
She wears the big, blue hat on the friendly street.
And isn't the brim wide enough to contain
Not only a carousel of every pleasure
But a millstone each of our duties
And all Saturn's lazy moons? Isn't she a proud and certifiable
                  Acolyte of redemption?

Here in the restaurant, one man admits,
As the regulars fork into their lunches
   (these geniuses of love extending dominions!)
That, since last Christmas, he's gone unkissed.
And it had been grandma, and now she's dead.
Meanwhile out there – you may as well know –
Beneath that hat, the woman's bare shoulder,
Ingenuously granted to a collective
   Is so sincere as to rebuff the breezes.

One Fine Summer

In those lovely evenings,
Each cloud a point of contact
With the setting light
Birds caught in their wings,
You thought it beyond words,
This something eternal for the moment,
The boughs rich with leaves.
In every eye was burning
The shadows of the world.
It was a fire, an ache
No face avoids.
And all of that completed
The ordinariness brought
    To a high incandescence.

        – It's how it was when the breeze
            Shook your window in its old frame.

    And the lovers
Gardened on the street,
Bought and sold their goods,
As a cabbie swore, as a beggar fumed,
As, bent over, a woman mooned the crowd
And checked out red highheels
To be cleared at a marked-down price.
Horns and whistles!
It's how it was, the light all that mattered
        as you turned
The yellowing, aromatic pages of a book – the hot skin,
        the lovebites!
The window banged in its cracked frame.
Leaves rubbed against the glass.
And you would think each rose had
Its infinitely various market,
    A store for every appetite.

The light of the evening was all that mattered.
It was a light irretrievable once spent.
And the continuing ache for change,
    Negotiating desire, added desire to its conquests.

You had to go out to see what was,
How in themselves light and change
        are truth and lie
Always building for release.
You had to go out to catch absolute words
    At the Café Roma in the neighbourhood.

        – Mario: 'Come' va?'
        Frank: 'Who wants to know?'

You had to go out to leave behind,
In a begonia-busy room, in a dusty, carpeted room
With splintered window jambs
The eternities of a Roman poet.
And sometimes, the skies were pearl-like
And light seemed to dream
As if major events were breaking
    And nothing would remain the same.

But by her window, Harriet stood over Patricia,
Removed the towel, combed the wet hair,
Held the girl's long, red hair
    Up to the passing day, supper on the stove.

They had pledged to hang about,
No reason for it but to shout
        down at a boy
Like yourself, 'Come on up! We've got lots!'
Drinks and gossip were faith's foundations,
And what, that evening, to believe
    And throw away as useless in the morning.

It might go well like this one year in a hundred,
Everyone a champion, no one claiming
    unique knowledge of
Lust, love, loneliness, – when all the smiles
Are as they should be, when skies shine like pearls
Though days unfetter themselves,
    Change and doom billions.

    – It's how it was by way of an edge
      In the wine, in the leaves, in the light,
        in the birds.

And you had to go out to see how it was,
Smell the relieving rain pouring down –
The summer all heat, wars, and women,
The trees lush, the young so anxious.
    So it was, one fine summer.

Isaac

Summer, and I cut across
The shadows of a street.
I am a number by which a sum of shadows
Increases or diminishes. And I am paler than a faith
That had the respect of kings.
I carry in my heart my father,
Some dim memory of his anguish.
If I were to ask a god's forgiveness
For the intent to sacrifice
The all-consuming memory,
The need would pass away
    And others take the place.

Say I am Isaac. I am no stranger to myself.
The world is all. I welcome the emissaries.
Those tourists on the terraces, those pigeons on a ledge,
That dog releasing urine
In a littered flower-bed . . .
A raucous parrot in its cage
Charms its merchant-keeper.
The leaves are hanging still
    In the windless air.

I walk along, my always anxious father
The offering in my heart,
Even as I – say I am Isaac – repudiate
The certainties of the young.
This flirtatious woman here! A tiny garden there
In which to woo her . . . Say I am Isaac who loves this
    Transfer of day to dark.

Now the yelling whore . . . A cabbie's squealing tyres . . .
A stench of pizza . . . And there's a need to embrace
And another that would deny –
Though it seems early yet, my father uneasy,
Me kicking up my heels –
    The shouts and the smells.

Childhood, so I remember,
Was no time of remorse.
Dispassionately, the children
Pursued their interests.
But say I am Isaac seeking
To isolate what my father saw,
Who with the eyes of a child
Already weary of a god
    Was peering into God.

Say, however, I may only know,
As the price of change, what changed.
Say I remember most
A surrendered street
And lovers on a motorbike.
Say the girl's skirt billows high,
Her hair a stream of rebuke,
    Old men in shadows muttering.

This night is hot by the St Lawrence.
It will be awhile before it cools
And one may think of sleeping,
Abraham still asking
Forgiveness of his god. Say Isaac makes his wonder,
'Why is it always this:
Always that sky torn
    From a rootless ground?'

And say it may end for the likes of me
When, above all else, God is loved
    As the reason there was for living, –

When the hands of the old are lonely,
When morning, noon, and night
And all the verities, when all
That had been for sure – :
The eleventh-hour eyes, the wild, disordered hair
In the starting up again with angels
So as to fail once more – when all this goes over
        to the unreliable young.

But say that I am Isaac. I am Isaac who laughs
As he was born of an old woman
To be his father's son. . . . But even so, say he finds
The night agreeable, the city spirited,
One that permits – despite the heat –
    Love, sacrifice, perversion, and more.

Going out on the town, I went looking for the affections.
It's a necessity on the frontier, the moon wedged between
    the clouds
Indifferent to the business. April and lilacs now
Bloom in their respective culverts
Of mind and real estate, the dull, rainy years endured.
What does the invitation always say?
    Time says, 'Come, renew your passage!'

And here's Ebie in her window, cigarette in hand,
As I return empty-handed
To the neighbourhood. And her good eye smiles and her bad eye
    glares
At the street. She waits tables on Europeans.
Afternoons, the titan sun
Sometimes loosens his yankee tongue
And licks her cheeks as though
    They were sugarcakes.

She waves me in, locks the door, sits me down.
She sets out glasses now, pours, and leans
Across the counter. There's a serious look to her.
Her breasts are still young and ripe
So she has always had me know.
'You listen to me,' she says
    Who has enjoyed her husbands.

It was war for me, the pitching of politics at love.
Sometimes one threw for strikes.
Some say the game's rigged even now.
Maidenly, pure – the dawn!
Patriarchal, dirty – the rag-end . . .
Anyway, for her, the market was the thing:
Brand new leather jacket
For the man of the hour,
Girlfriends supplying her with dainties
    by way of gift exchanges.

And now I'll hear for the rest of my life Ebie's
      harsh advice.

   Or when a dry spell withers the plain, the predators –
In search of food – attack
What, in better times, they leave unmolested:
Those pale, hedonistic Celtic souls
    Grazing on the sidewalk.

   Yet with that smirking look Ebie gets
When back in Budapest or in Las Vegas
She sits and is admired for her patience
At the pool, it's odd how she lets me hear
Not what I should do
But that she liked
Childhood's snowy hills, childhood's ice-bound lakes,
    Horses pulling, sleigh bells ringing – stories her mother told.

   – The limousines are floating by,
Gassed and pretty girls hollering out.
But the moodier women who can't be had until they've got you
Take the bus: isn't that Molly – her head bowed –
Doing penance to her body
    That a loser caressed it?

   There it is, that most selfish act. It has no room for base
      selfishness,
And yet, love is time. Love does not cleave from time
    If the greed come modestly.

   So, perhaps, it isn't so strange at all, Ebie and me
Dancing to an orchestra: for now, no loneliness, no history,
No boys spinning around with bullets in them,
No girls bedding the liberators – as was the case with our parents
    and theirs.
I have been obsessed, looking for ways to belong somewhere
And here it had nearly slipped my mind
    (it would only take five minutes) to enter a familiar place
      and drink
A toast with Ebie. So I tell her
    I am leaving town for good.

But then when she believes me and fiercely plants her kiss
And reconstructs my face
And carves her soul on mine
With her heart's penknife,
And a consummation building
Catches me unawares, then emotions flow –
Those pale things wanting air
As they ask: 'What's all this? We didn't think ourselves
      appropriate
Objects of your corrective design!'
Her good eye smiles.
Her bad eye glares: 'What's there to know?'
Then it's over – in that unlit, smoky hole.
Me and her . . .
    We were always like brother and sister.

August Kranz

Even now I have not done with it.
So much goes beyond politics, the corrupt and the good
        intent
Agitating in the mind like pistons.
Father rode out his end.
At the wheel of his cab, objective, he cruised
Rain-slick streets of bad parts of town
For the better part of a million miles
        And took sides when it suited him.

Mother lifted and pressed down her iron.
She pushed it across the family linens.
They were always adding to my emptiness: father's distance,
        mother's time
That was an infinitely round place.
Some nights, on the kitchen table she laid
Sheets of crisp, blue paper,
Then sat, sighed, and developed
        A tension in her brain.

She would rhyme words she shouldn't
On the thin vellum, move heaven and earth
To tell a story. Her agony was the view if her talent lied.
        It was a sore that festered the more she worked the
            membrane.

It was stretched across what the eyes might see
And the means she had to argue with it, the moon shining
Or the rain slanting down.
A collection of glassware
Bivouacked on the shelves,
Vessels from which fumes
Had once widened nostrils,
        Were an army of her faithful.

Her love was meant to drive
The treacheries from the field.
But in the meantime one heard out
The best explanations, the vaguest proofs,
And the excuses least likely to explain anything, –
And fed husband and child, and ironed,
In medicinal glass tried to catch
    The pursued or the master in oneself.

And the cold moon glowed white or the rain pelted leaves,
    Those maples stable in her trance.

This father whose bowels were bilious,
This mother sweet on her experiments,
Named me. So far, August Kranz
    Has not matched with much. . . .

★

I went to work at Dispatch. And when no other employable
        misfit,
Overly zealous about the rules, was breathing down my neck,
On the sly I got father fares. It helped him pay
    The office fees. After college, I booked a plane.

It was a mistake to fly. I had always dreamed of distant
        places,
But while the engines whine, you just count the seconds. You arrive,
        at last,
No different than when you left.
I settled on Paris,
Wound up in a verminous room,
    Loathe to remove my shoes.

Still, it was time to begin distrusting
The heroes who didn't matter, who couldn't matter, who were
        substitutes
For those who had always mattered. So whether or not it was
        a dream I had

In which all good men and women carry the day
And beauty's the measure, something broke open my urges
    And in vehement chorus showed me a way.

    'Awgoost, Awgoost . . .'
It started one night
As I climbed the stairs to fetch my key.
    'Awgoost . . .' I heard.

    In the way that actors
Would defy every kind of weather, rumbling in their carts along
        the roads,
Pressing on – with their mise en scenes –
    To the next engagement, so these voices clattered through me.

    The door, slightly ajar, by which I stood
Was always closed
On a mysterious cubicle, room of plants and cheap Renoirs,
        the woman discreet
    Who handed out keys and messages.

    'Awgoost! See her in her soft things,
She just about to spark
The man sobbing in her lap, the wink for you?
Yet there's nobility to her suitor's pathetic ways:
Desperate, he'll let her drive
His Mercedes, – he'll raise her station in life a notch
If she'll come across. Awgoost!
The space of which you are a part contracts
    To the blazing, blue coals of her eyes!'

    – Who but the old man I will become
Will care to remember I have chased time
Along the infinite promise of her lineaments
    And drowned in her sweet hair?

★

Dad pimped.
He drove a cab. His heart seized, he died at the wheel.
Maybe, that was politics: his straw-straight hair mussed,
Eyes still concealing their intelligence
Of rage in people, danger in transport.
The three whores who hailed him, a summer night's business
        in the offing,
Got out, and flagged the competition
    And so, kept with the faith. Convenience rules.

    – The news reached me and no tinder struck
Between man and woman, no name called out
In the heat of an afterthought,
No hot loveliness cupped in a hand
    Put right my father's end.

*

    Mother took to drink, smoke, and meat.
Save for the kitchen, she closed off rooms,
Said, 'Nebuchnednezzar', said 'Judith' –
Anything to complicate rhyme, to make difficult her grief.
It was the guilt of the artist.
She applied make-up to her face.
It had once been plain, uncomplicated.
The little mole on her chin had always supported three black
        hairs.
Sometimes, her brown eyes seemed to turn a golden colour
        in her dollop of time.

    Hers was the theatre of a recluse,
The revenge of a cast-off slipper.
Happiness expires, – flesh decays.
In her best china teapot she kept the proofs:
    The ashes of her husband.

*

I flew back, returned to Dispatch
And at my old position took my loss, and through clenched teeth
        still managed
To call out the number of suite or house, call for the car in trouble
And pass the details to the cops.
    Though it was unwanted, I regained the town's pulse.

    Mother brought home more troops, one army of glass not enough,
The iron stone cold, the thin, blue sheets of paper wasted.
    It wasn't going well. And I sat with old men in doomed hotels.

    The rapture and cowardice, mediocrity, defeat,
The shrugging shoulders, also are
Ghosts of the mind that shape us.

    In a Paris parlour the furniture was
A copy of past days, the woman too good
What with the passions she spent, the clothes she purchased
        at heroic sacrifice,
    She the prime cost-factor.

    Even now I have not done with it, how madame's missing molar richly
Supplied her smile its fulness,
    And the tryst, when it sprung, loosened her tongue.

    'Child, I am always depressed,
But I am entranced by your face:
Exaggerated, it's almost beautiful.'
'Awgoost!' chimed the chorus. A sweet rest
Would follow the sweet attentions
    And affection soar.

    Even now the memory – a blue glass of sleep –
Forms the only god I make: her lips relaxed with their mixed
        chatter,
Her eyes at peace, her 'Mon dieu, caro mio,
    You are a friendly putz!'

    – And even now I thank her: 'You took me as good-natured,
    Nothing in my head but argument.'

                    ★

The Slavic beauty . . .
She left at dawn.
    She, new-found companion, had stayed the week.

*

It is one thing to be shot out of the air,
Revelation fishtailing through the brain,
Leaving no trace save a smoking smile,
But it's quite another to have words,
To engage too quickly the trial of love
    With the god who is everywhere but is absent from us
        absolutely.

It is to say she may no longer visit, insinuate her ungainly form
Into a lesser mortal's room,
Her proud limbs as wracked as a medieval
    Carving, her long toes a ballet.

Once she was a shadow's shadow, an ancient, now interrupted
Egotism. And here I had thought she was captivated
    By the cruel circus in my heart.

She'd kneel beside me, agreeable, prayerful, a deep cunning
    To the grin on her face.

Now gone to her early morning dispatch shift
She'll answer phones and make her tallies
Of cigarettes, chocolates, diet cokes
    To go to whores and pimps in basements.

SeaVue Apartments! The view in places
Is obscure and blocked in others.
And the rooms reek of beer, fish, cabbage, onions.
No one who lives here leaves for long
    Unless they prefer Winnipeg as a grave.

31

As continually as the cabs keep calling,
The occupants shuffle cards, uncap the beers
While I sleep and sometimes wonder
  How it goes with mother.

Sleep is precious. It rebuilds the self, even as, in others,
It postpones refurbishing. Down the street – the hydrangeas neglected,
The fence picturesque – mother can't help but suspect
That verse won't bring her happiness
  As it gangs up on her.

At dawn she left – my debutante.
She was a cool Persephone colouring her lips
And running out the door,
  Tickled pink with herself.

Where we sprout ears an ageless god –
Or so a story tells it – spreads his wings. And the way Sleep flees us
  Is how Sleep listens to our piecemeal dreams.

In a few hours, at Dispatch, I will be answering phones – in the union.
I will get the judge's widow to the hairdresser.
I will direct the hooker back from the suburbs.
I will field the complaint of the woman late for the concert:
'The driver lacked change . . . he needs a bath . . .
  Where do you find them?'

I will put my feet into socks, frame into a suit,
Remember Heraclitus said this, Plato that
And Lenin plotted. But saddled with agriculture,
'Awgoost' farms cabs, forms a god, and the time
  Is never his to keep.

I will turn on the gas, boil the water,
Wait on the toast, go to the bookshelf:
  Gaius Suetonius Tranquillus? Or Evelyn St John Waugh's nasty prose?

I will lean out the window and drink the coffee
And catch hints of the Ineffable:
The landlord's vines stale in the wind,

32

A rusted gashog up on blocks,
Clouds gathering over, building for rain,
Two drunks putting knockout moves
    On the busstop bench, the coast an apparition, citizens
        a mist.

    I will order in, tonight, from the 'Golden Dragon',
For I will have worked my shift,
Fought the fight of virtue with a girl.
    Pardon then, my theology.

    But I say to the 'I am that I am'
'You are that You are', and all of the realm:
Kitchen table, bare light bulb,
That spoon longing for its Canaan,
That photo, too: mother and father 'Just Married'
    Drift against my jaw. Otherwise, what's new?

    That to my fathers I, curly-haired, bear no likeness?
That madness closes in on mother
    From out of Sleep's lovely blue glass?

    Even now I have not done with it:
How mother was vain and father vicious,
How politics is just a way of keeping score
As angels select partners, – how, in the combat
Sparks are struck, go flying everywhere.
But if a dreamer believes he has
Added to the divine discharge,
    The spectacle is only one of sport.

    'Awgoost! Awgoost!' it goes all day
And night. A tease. A palimpsest.
And heaven and earth, it seems,
    Move of their own accord.

The Emperor's Best Friend, Michael Psellus

Of course, in Plato, there are fine things,
But I like horses better. Christ is grand, too, and Homer
    and the poets,
But I in my sprawling kingdom
  Loved the sport of the bed.

Psellus refined me, held out to me
The old lore of rule and wise stewardship.
I learned historians began accounts
With their places of origin, their modest family
    backgrounds.
  I have watched my friend peddle gossip.

Still, Basil did this and Justinian that
    according to
Some caress of the mind.
I believe. Yea, I believe.
Even as I am laid up, even as I am not cold
To the fine things in Plato, to Homer and the poets,
To the conquering Christ. My cough is as dry as a bag
    of beans,
My laughter more so. I think that with life
  I am finished.

And I think that the winter sun
Sits here neutral with me
In the room, my attendants impassive, their private
    quarrels with God
None of my concern. Outside, the trees are waiting, too,
Like all proofs of God that wait
And are disowned, – while men of mine build my parks
And women of mine brew herbs
  For the Saviour in their quarters.

Psellus, I understand, is on the way,
Has, of late, been eating lentils
In the monastery. He has been dulling his sins and coarsening his
    existence
With gristly lumps of meat.
Did he go there of his own volition?
   Did I condemn him?

I think God, nature, men and women
In their totalities and relations
Are riddles. Yet it's clear my ambitious, weak, and
     nasty friend
Was born for the life that thrives
   On a high, intellectual plane.

And he will enter his own house once more and not know it.
He will address the familiars and not know them.
He will beg a meal, pry loose a penny,
Their pride sheltered, his worth nothing.
The man will barely notice the time infecting
Living tissue and mind, so intent he will be on the
    recompense due him
For service to God and state. Shall I raise him up again?

The mumbling priest makes love to my dying.
Winter out there and I go
As sleet attacks the land. And Psellus comes
Straightaway from Narsou, from the layabouts of the place
Where he knows a thing or two more than them.
I prefer a scoundrel's laughter.
Knowledge? I think the wind that kisses the sea
   Is hardly less melancholy than I.

   – I think I loved most a clown
Who spoke as children prattle.
   He almost stole the government.

I see it now, Psellus waved through the halls, –
Psellus alarmed the hour's my last, but already scheming
Though I have arranged for my successor.

Flesh that must eat and occupy space
Resents lack. Appeals to the spirit, should things go wrong,
Show a shaky hand and mark the end
Of getting things done. Psellus, of course, will
      always pray
  It won't come to that.

  And what does it all mean?
It means, I think, that a wind kisses the sea
And Pythagorean numbers rattle in the brain
      like beans,
Gently but insistently, as though scattered by a
      hand
    In a kind of benediction.

  It means that when the story has been told, most men
Will be caught out and seen
    To have inclined to the worse.

  It means my subjects lived and died. It means I fared
      well
In some years and poorly in others, laughing through
      my ailments,
Shrugging off errors made
On the long and twisted road of government
That would run like a broad avenue through the
      land.
It means who better than Psellus knows my nature,
    Pleasures, secret cares?

  It means that, rising in the east, the sun begins there
      its journey
Around our fixed point
And expects to ignite
Each and every desire
And then drag its leg through the filth.
  It means that when Psellus was teaching me
The arts of statecraft,
    Child tolerated child.

It means that, in the way, on a winter field,
Shadow moves across snow,
His thought moved on mine, and yet
We are each our own quality
And everything's theatre unless, brutal enough,
Theatre spares no secret.

I am afraid my friend will arrive too late.
Who knows where I go?
I think that's sun on the vines
And peace on the land.

Michael Psellus: AD 1018-96. Byzantine philosopher, historian, man of letters.

Constantine IX, who was said to have admitted the marketplace rabble into the senate, reigned between 1042-1055.

Spice

When I could I watched her
Work the terraces of the boulevard
Among the world travellers
And carriers of new tales.
To best treat a hangover
Or jetlag in California, you go and look
For a hole in the wall.
In Nepal you do the same.
One heard these comments. Singular in the crowd,
Spice had gone nowhere.

*

The ships are rotting in the harbours.
The crews are potted in the bars,
Dead to the old persuasions
To sail off and retrieve a girl. Her prince rummages
In VideoMovieLand, brushfires smoking in him
Set by his own hand. He has his dignity:
When woman measures man for a void
Love's universe is honoured.

*

But Spice was not one to languish, not with her looks,
Though she was often separate, the sun's favourite
When she approached the tables of the learned.
Affairs had to be brief affairs
To best suit Spice: the give and take of humiliation, –
Stellar acts of theatre then
Perfectly executed, quickly forgotten,
Her genius, her fragile
Sense of herself.

*

Their faces smooth and tanned,
Their eyes studious and opaque,
Guarantors of respectability, prime pickings for Spice,
Men heard out her fears.
Then Spice shut the door on them,
She as fickle as a cat, the lovemaking hearkening back
          to another age.

     – We used to say: 'Let's go see Spice! To hell
          With everyone else!' We went.

★

She had looks, oh perhaps not those
That might launch a thousand ships, today,
But of the profiles she granted us
     One was always exquisite. It showed she was perverse.

And when one slept with her,
And if you were one like me
Who on occasion ponders
     What does it mean – :

    'Better alienated of riches,
     Than of an unexamined life, take the pauper's lot' – :

When one, inconsolable, laid down with Spice,
One bedded the secure capitols
Of a generous country. There were always those other
Well-defended contenders
Winning more time to themselves
     Than one might believe necessary.

    But will we hear no more of Spice?

★

Who was lovely to behold, her eyes wide
With disintegrations, she herself trading in
   The vouchers of fulfilment.

   How Spice with white cloths at her places of work
Rubbed long-stemmed glasses free of dust
All the while telling us
She had passed her tests
   And would go into real-estate.

   We would say: 'Let's go see Spice.'
When our futility appalled even us, it was:
'Let's go get Spiced.' And she would say,
'When I am rich I will see to you.
I will invite you to my parties
And set you among the captains of every field
   So long as it amuses.'

*

   One does not love for the sake of love
         but for a bliss
Stolen from the space and time of promise.
And we worshippers of Spice
Were corrupt and we were vague
And effete, though – given the grotesque hour –
   We hardly need be more material.

   Such a nose she had!
      That dimpled chin . . .

   'Go for it!'
'Hold nothing back. Sting the bastards, their original
         sin, their
Besetting faux pas
They are so nice.' A day would come
   And she'd have no use for us.

*

Love Spice? We adored her!
But of all her moods, there was one
I kept my distance from, – and her laughter flashed
    across her lips
Like lightning in a cloud.
The man might reason it out like this,
Watching her bring a plate of something,
Seated round the table
A congenial, upscale crowd: relinquish wisdom, spurn power,
Scorn riches, spite fame
On her account? Of course not.
And she would walk away, tugging on the cross
Ornate and heavy on her blouse,
    Her eyes grey, silent, avaricious.

A Beautiful Kingdom

Surrounded by the riches, the monumental detail
　　　of the capitol,
There to sack it, he on his first tour
Was quick to realize
His importance. He was neither the structure nor the shadow
　　　of it all,
Unaccounted for. Cold nights on the way,
　　The leaves beginning to present their pageant . . .

Surrounded by the riches, the monumental detail
　　　of the repaired capitol,
Some barbarians stay. And sooner or later, the waiters
Get insolent, the napkins creased just so again
In the long-stemmed glasses.
They look as though they are about to fly, these pure birds
　　　announcing
　　To sea-weary sailors the presence of landfall.

Cakes, tortes, croissants, black breads,
The cheeses and the sausages, the coffee brewing (the aroma
　　　excellent),
Strawberries and cream, too, punctuate the muted talk
In a grand hangout. Its object: the elusive self.
To this a fellow from the sticks
　　Ought to prefer the loud democratic mayhem
　　　of smoky taverns.

Astonished, at first, to find
Certain closed societies permeable,
He unfolds a newspaper, – he brushes a lone piece
　　　of lint
From his sleeve. With ease he handles the inquisitory arrows
Of women of rank, and yet, the waiter draws around this
　　　impetuous specimen
A cautionary quarantine. It does not deny service
　　But it suggests what one's not.

– Drizzly day. The wet white oaks.
The Paris ham on a baguette.
      Crisp lettuce. Rather dear.

   The biting autumn air brings to him
Free-floating memory. The years had travelled barbarian-style
      through all that time,
Through the ransacked geographies of sex.
Now who gets what? In what measures, in which hour?
He ought to know: few lovers, crossing one's path,
      mark the place
For future reference. His crown of experience is
      as encrusted,
   As ornate as any ceremonial gold.

   If material spoils aren't enough, the imagined life has
      its treasures.
From a high brow she will have pulled back her hair,
And it will seem to accentuate her eyes
And the memories therein – this aristocrat of knowing
   What it meant to lose much.

   She will seem to have dropped down
From a place high on the social scale, the surrounding park's
      lovely trees
Resplendent in their autumn vestments, – and she will seem unsuited
      for the ground now,
And the perfectly capable waiter, on purpose, will misconstrue
Her biscuits, her tea for a pretender's.

   'But you,' she will say, addressing her companion while
Labouring hard to imagine herself
In the palace again, 'You should consider yourself
      fortunate:
The ripple you are is so far removed
From the point of initial disturbance to the empire
You are one with the centre and easy with the edge.
You are the barely perceptible agitation
   Of an ornamental pond.'

There will be books in this woman! History! Well might she ask
    of her ageless enemies:
'Who has such contempt for disorder my foes are left
    To wander hells familiar to them?'

Well might she ask: 'And wasn't that Homer selling bright balloons
To victory's soldiers in the bombed square?
The way he shuffles around the splendours and ruins
    And celebrates every feast.'

But after awhile, he ceases trying
To impress this the latest one
Sent to examine him for weaknesses,
Even as she loses interest.
He jaws away on his sandwich, the issues of the intellect
    of no concern now.
Well might he say to the grief and the hatred established
    In the woman's stony eyes:

'Submit to the seasons, to cycles of gain and loss.
Then your suppurating wounds may close.
Then self-punishment may go less severe.
When hearts are given to the conquering passions of the quiet
    pagan,
Of the pious Christian, ideas take them.
    Life's a business.'

And in the form of a rare mist, the rain outside clings
    to vines,
To the bright taxis, to the women in elegant footwear, to the
    laughing, uptown men.
Well might he say to the woman of the imagined life,
'Should you not like anything much now
Of what you see around you, give me your body.
    We will be intimate.'

After awhile, bored with no one in particular:
With himself, with his companion, with the exhausted civility
    of waiters,
He explains: 'They were my fathers, men in whom

Ruin spread. Some left and bridged
To other lands. But never mind. Make any mistake with me you like.
   When the bloom's worn off the cure, even I can be generous.'

   After awhile, through a trick of time, or simply because
He starts to keep to himself too much, lovers and loners whisper
Their ridicule in his ear: 'Balloon, mein Herr, balloon?'
That sad, old baritone! It's the destroyer.
   It's life's sweetness.

   As the woman of the imagined life fades away,
Walking slow along the boulevard
Of shadow and structure
Back to rooms where she has no one
With whom she might be severe,
Leaving the waiter a compensatory tip
For the fuss she had caused, the barbarian remonstrates
         with himself:
'For the pains I underwent to get here and remain
   And repair, I might have had that dish of sliced peach.'

The still beautiful Mrs Orlow drew
The curtains in her shop. Snow fell in the early evening.
It was going to be five o'clock.
No time-piece in Mrs Orlow's shop
Ever tells the time correctly.

My love kissed me in our room
       above Mrs Orlow's shop.
I smiled through the benefice
As though to kiss like that
And not better the world
       were dangerous.

To Mrs Orlow come
These heavily rouged widowers! They hobble in
Wishing to have objects fixed
In which a heart invested love
Or a declaration of the thing
       strong enough
To weather time's breakages.

Yes, there is tumult in the perennial kiss.
There are unstable felicities
Wanted and sometimes, gotten.
Even in the poorest city, kisses are plentiful,
Though a widower say, 'They're not!'
And on a menacing cane,
Grumpy, wheel about
In Mrs Orlow's shop.

Snow fell in the early evening.
It was going to be five o'clock.
Confident, I went down the stairs,
Saw Mrs Orlow reaching up. As she drew the curtains shut
With such a feminine flourish
I thought the gesture mystical.

How well I might have believed
In a decline and fall of things,
Of a spirit that left the world
Not to return, and yet my love's
Lips had been moist, her eyes far-seeing!

Perhaps, God never had business here.
Perhaps, we vibrate until disconnected,
The best lie of which a social order
       has the use
Uncoupling some good sport's worst truth
      from himself.
Yet, like a troubadour who would prove
Devotion through his deeds of valour – my transport, my defence
But childhood's improvisations – I was stepping out
To get the makings of a supper.

And all the while I was thinking
Love behaves like love
  (just as any object
  fills its space), I knew I was but
    a wretched creature
In the old religious sense.
Goodness will manufacture,
In its own image, goodness
Though love is aggression out there, –
Good would drown the world
In its bullying ways. It was going to be five o'clock
And sincerity fatal
And light still light
At the edge of the dark.

Love behaves like love. It is what it is
Just as lamb I found, costing much, was meat, – just as there
    seemed
No frozen peas to be had
    conveniently anywhere.
It was going to be five o'clock
In the Hanseatic League of the galactic heart.

It was going to be just about that time, the physics doomed.
Religion, politics, state, all that?
Worms are it.

Still, man, woman, child,
Given reasons to trade, would continue to construct their trading
        posts
As best they could.
And love behave like love
And Mrs Orlow draw her curtains
And her time-pieces tell time wrong,
Falling farther and farther away from God
To her girlish purview.
Those curtains shut, would she slide into her slippers
        first,
Then pour herself a small reward? Would she let it lapse
That power's the clout
In the hands of the few and the many?
It was snowing, at any rate.

The still beautiful Mrs Orlow drew
The curtains in her shop. Snow fell in the early evening.
It was going to be five o'clock.
And yet, no time-piece of hers
Ever keeps up with itself.

A Woman Reading Genesis

She is in her lovely night.
Countless fires breathe above.
They are the silken galaxies
That canopy the hills around.
She in her house, blooms surrounding,
The windows as warm as skin
Though love is cold, at the kitchen table sits.
She made room for the book
     To which her shoulders slope.

And her hair is newly frosted.
Her nails are polished mauve.
How things turn out! That she should sit
And read what she reads
While bugs bang the glass
Of apertures in the walls.
The dead her audience, the script untried
Though many have tried it and got bigotry,
Born for the stage, she presents herself
To the badlands. Genesis.
     The heart's ghostly park.

God and devil scored man's mind.
Man carved the earth to suit himself.
Yet come the sweetest pleasure and the blackest pain,
Who owns the evening?
'There was a blinding light.
Then the effect wore off,
And history had a name
And the name its history.
All that lies in shadow now.'
When she asks, in this way I give
Rome and agriculture,
Rome and the City of Heaven,
Her arthritic finger crooked
     Between some pages of the book.

Tailless, web-footed things
Are chorusing, fireflies in the weeds.
Cars scatter gravel on the road.
'Don't stop,' she'll say. 'No treats.'
She sends the smoke of cigarettes
Across the book's harsh themes
And splashes sour wine
Into the unwashed cups.
But before her most expressive mouth
She piously holds a chocolate.
It's a spy at heathen gates
    Bidden to ransack a tooth. . . .

And it's a gently rising swell,
A wave rolling with deeps:
The steepness one ascends
To reach her in her refuge.
Here I had come the distance
Through beauty and through terror
I thought died with childish things,
And she left me out there to cool my heels
    While I knocked at the door.

Well, what would I bring
But a passing acquaintance with the hills?
From the pastures what was there to steal?
The summer shadows, themselves,
Are stealth upon the maples.
Their grip increasingly tight
In the warm, immodest wind,
They said, 'We formed the childhood.
    Childhood bred the sceptic.'

Or, under the old heaven-parts,
As one continues along the road to her,
One may call the good corrupt, the bad good.
Then as values crash
  (as one reaches the shack
    where, once yearly, hymns are sung)
    One honours the buggered god. . . .

*

She, born to easily cry
Under the sweet spell of a wine,
Is in her lovely night –
Planets glowing above,
    Things crawling below.

She who in her large beauty
Houses vast guilts,
Because desire is still regularity,
Because desire is virtue,
    Reads, cries, consumes.

My part in the game is to lend
Her the use of my eyes.
How lightly fingered, how generously drained
The chocolate and the cup! How lonely
    The flesh and the book!

'You join the drifters.
You debate the sleepless kings.
You were a child and are a woman.'
And she throws up her heavy hands. I am worse
    Than that other snake in the grass.

But as birds with rapid wings
Flit from branch to twig
So, in talk, premonitions speed
From light to dark: possibly,
    We are always mistaken. . . .

And the night spreads now – tree to tree.
A three-part myth: god, devil, man
Deepens the wine in our blood. That we are alone.
That we are loved, that we can't avoid
    Weaving patterns from the shadows.

Memory

The leaves heaped here
And there in sad piles
Just barely are the season –
Autumn on the boulevards.

And girls up from the metros,
Lighting smokes on the run,
Help glorify the affair,
  Girls going where they go.

And the living argue with the living
And the dead with the dead:
How a thing starts,
  How a thing ends – :

  Those names on the war-stones,
    Those skies the leaves brush,

  Those streets of happy windowshoppers,
    Those windblown newspapers.

  And a self that receives its image
    Has looked for the even more spectral.

  Still, these oaks, these wreathed memorials, these
        nanny-pushed
Prams, – and each love and each cruelty there was,
Each flung football
Spiralling over the fallen leaves –
All of it would retrieve
The aristocracies
  Of durations gone transparent.

First Things

The snow disappeared,
A breeze the persuasion,
May submits the campaign.
And with shimmering breasts, red-rimmed eyes,
Like dervishes the pigeons spin
On the grassy patches
  Of the shabby park.

And the cars gleam on streets that, yesterday,
Were caked with mud and salt.
Weather was a partner in all one did.
There's snow yet to smell in the air.
Boughs bare of leaves
Spider the ground with shadows,
    The grey trees still winter's.

★

They sit, heads bowed in laughter:
Girls are eating lunch in May.
They expose what they can of themselves to the sun,
    Side by side on the benches.

In session they condemn and forgive
Until clouds again bring gloom
And boys transparent promises.
It seems they haven't talked and thought things through
    All winter, so fast the words spill from their mouths.

★

Shod in worn runners,
Some passing a bottle,
With bellies given to the fire,
Blotchy skin to the sun,
    Old men gaze at these young.

And those of the old who aren't rambling
Too far out of their minds
Perhaps see in loveliness
    What used to wind away from them

As January blew snow and April poured rain
And August scorched. Women they would have liked to possess
    Tossed guilt, not bliss.

★

But then, on her haunches, bleary-eyed,
A woman who hasn't slept for days
Dangles a cigarette between her knees.
She looks too directly at the sky.
She asserts the authority
Of a hard time had, her battalions there
    But inconspicuous.

★

I can only put
My best face on my ignorance.
    There were two ordering principles to what was:

That love raises heaven beyond the sun,
That nemesis rights those too strong and blind
Should a life or a state collapse
Under the weight of emptiness.
In this way a matter of faith
    Appeared to take part in a cycle:

That the sun warms and the birds preen.
And women are serious even when casual.
And traffic must move and loners reabsorb
    What failure they can:

That grey and bare
        (the shadows still short
        of summer's rich shade)
The trees seem to disbelieve
            These sleepers, tipplers, lunchhour girls.

    It's partly the weather, I think —
The days still staggering into the clear
Along with the discontented voices.
It's how it is, this letting one another know —
As one jokes or just sits and stares —
        Of all that can yet go wrong.

Hattie's Visitor

Leave there! So what that it's cold
And the wind slams around, some limb on the roof
Scratching shingles with dead fingers.
If you're looking to be warm,
She in her bed wouldn't know
A tumble now, would she?
    Her breasts are loners.

    You, you may depart
Through a loose window,
Through a chink in the boards
Of the house. Why hang about in a sulk
And judge the mess?
She is not your girl though once she was.
And the room
    It will stay as it is.

    She knows, doesn't she know
How thin the world has become,
Thick parts uninhabitable,
Dials set to doom. Where would you take her, lord master?
What mover's van could handle
The load, the chaos of her years, postcards insisting:
'Hattie, come join us!'
(in London or Corfu),
    Postcards signing off: 'Cheers!'

    With you an affectionate moment
Always gave her pause.
It was like crossing the border. 'Anything to declare?'
Your hands used to start fast, then run out of gas,
So many ghosts to guard against.
You, a gentleman, pretended her perfect.
    She hadn't the patience.

And the air you had her breathe! it was no less
Than the waitingroom humour of *Reader's Digest*,
And God laughed gently
At the best lines
Small lives rate. She stirs now in her sleep.
Take a number. The moon and the wind,
The road winding through the hills
    Empty in her bed.

    Liar, the very air lies and withers truth.
Oh, she is charity itself, if an innocent
Who shall not bend and touch her toes,
Let alone outrun competitors,
Land the contract, close the deal.
She'll not dazzle juries, terrify witnesses,
Tweak the judge, lunch on asparagus.
    She hasn't the patience.

    She has prayed, she certainly has
For love, a ravisher
With pleasing limbs and sparkling eyes
Walking unconcerned to her. And she is what you lost,
She with her silly hats, she spilling Triple XXX
On a lecher's lap. She's the moon and the snow.
She's the road in the hills.
    She's defined there in her bed.

    Prayed, and you appeared.
She got you to hold
And feel life drain from her.
Evenings now, she in a chair
    (and how it sags), curls her tongue around chocolates
And brushes out her tresses, and expects an episode
To knock down the familiar moon
    As she gives Arts and Entertainment respect.

    The words yelled in anger,
In sorrows, in fun . . . that's how people are.
It offends you still. Her farmers, her carpenters, her bingers and wives
Awake in the crypt of marriage

Maximize cruelties and torment the hills
Even when dead. She, too, prefers every cowardice
To that hell of making a difference.
　　She hasn't the patience.

　　　　Come on, man, take a stab!
Poor you. Things just might go wrong
As you impose, as you in a hundred ways abuse her
With sins you can't admit you own,
Then cuddle, then sever relations
With events long and wide with crime,
All the while (you thoughtful) you cry on her twin splendours
　　So as to succeed and, oh you god! save Hattie.

　　　　Alright then. But in the morning, you go.
Sleep. Sin hard, champion.
Take to your post.
Be the moonlight, the snow,
The road winding through the hills
And the animals come down
　　To test the place.

When Nero, young consul, still amiable,
Established relations with the girl,
It was Spring and it was morning
And they were fooling by the pool.
She leaned back on her haunches.
She brushed hair from her eyes.
    'You are close to dying,' she said.

Nero, young consul, still amiable,
Before the blackness lit his mind
  (he would bring a New Age to Rome),
Scrutinized her golden eyes for trouble –
This slave from the mountainous orient,
Her tribe famous for the ecstasies
That were its religion. And he could see in her jest no undoing,
No assassin in the employ of a rival
    And so, just thought her high-spirited.

Nero replied, 'It is proper season
For you and I to offend my forebears
And their gods. Exotic flowers surround us.
Caged birds sing. The mirrors shine with our bodies.
That I toy with a strand of your hair,
Twisting it around my finger to pull
Your lips closer to mine
Is only my way to propitiate
My desire not to die. I awoke this morning joyful,
With so much generosity
For every thing alive.
    I wonder if something's newborn in me?

It might be a god, I say to you,
Of fresh and clear complexion
Who, wagering with his beloved
    Brothers and sisters, says,

"Look at Nero, born to a creep and a bitch
Under such bad omens, nine months after
Tiberius croaked. I will encourage his worst tendencies.
    My dears, I will make him a poet."

    Will you laugh at me, girl, and tell me,
"Be manful. Earn your glory?"
Do you worry that the house I will construct for you
Of gold, silver, and marble
May provoke the old heaven, irritate the stars
Into which my genius flies
    As unerringly as any hero's spear?

    How now you tremble before my name!
Think of it! Nero loves a slave.
He would reverse order and crown her queen.
They aren't true, you know, the rumours out there.
My stars are the best and brightest fate.
They are those of a poet, and we will seat poetry
    In the imperial chair.'

    Then he kissed her, – the girl blushed,
Embarrassed for him by the claims he spoke
Such as can't be made, no, not even from
One soon to be Caesar. This demented, young man . . .
    How would she ever be secure?

That Sort of Woman, This Kind of Place

She is the sort of woman who,
In this kind of place
Of emigrés, of petty profiteers, is no one you'd think
    special
Until suddenly, you notice,
Nothing else panning out.
And she holds a mirror to her face.
It does not concern her much –
What the Serb goes on about.
His booming voice carries far,
His fork and knife precise, his thoughts, too,
Concerning Europe. Magda, married, says she's not,
And men are always undressing
The pleasant woman,
    Hearts thudding with disappointment.

    Lunchhour finished, the kitchenmaid
Regains the dining area.
She lights a cigarette, – she scrutinizes the stolen property
The sailor just brought in.
On display there are
        (the items spread across the table
        like an arrested man's effects) – :

    A gold bracelet, digital watches,
Queen-sized bedsheets, a track suit – polyester.
The steak knives are top of the line. And the teddybear's
    good
For a budding materialist.

    Well, the proprietor lipreads the racing form.
Everyone already has
One of everything, – the thief, undaunted, repacks
The loot. Magda sits there lonely, a soft material
Brushing her newly invincible breasts.
It has often seemed like home, this clearinghouse,
Though the proprietor will often miss

61

Old King Stephen's crown.
Innocents here irk him, the way they keep deriving solace
          from substitutes.

     'I like a building with character.
I love old cities. Budapest. Rome' –
Magda's voice so thin, as insubstantial
As the light of the cold, October sun.
If you begin to consider her sensible, a woman who knows
          the world,
Still, you'll start to wonder how you may best court her:
With battered façade, angles out of true?

     Now there's shouting on the street:
'Hey man! Let's meet at Danny's.
We'll hork us down refreshments.'
Leaves scuttle across the sidewalk.
Old feet unshape tennis shoes, young feet shod in cults.
Magda's subtle complexion, luminous eyes,
Little red round mouth . . . you'll wonder, too, just where you
          are
In a ghostly procession of orders,
Cradle and grave in sight. Ernie, nudging your shoulder, says,
'Magda likes to dance.'

     And the thief walks out of the place
With a rolling seaman's gait,
The cap cocky on his head.
In the sky, a lone bird wheels off.
The sailor's the sort who never loses:
The earth neither burns nor drowns for him.
It just bumps and grinds its way
Through the days and night, while some stars belch gases
And others inhale them.
And we're swept along, the failures pleasant, not bad here,
          like the meals.
Magda's breath
Sour with cigarettes and sweet with
          girlishness
     Washes against my face.

She asks, 'What are you always thinking?'
She almost seems entertained, hers the sort of voice
That, when it speaks, drains the mind of silence
Through the drawing power of sympathy.
So that the thought I had in me recedes, the hold it had
        now broken,
The image it would get right
Some thorny bush, the kind of redemption that grows
        On the edge of every precipice.

    The kitchenmaid, returned to work, frying meat on the grill,
With subterranean voice,
Hums a song, and the proprietor – he who has no use for faiths
At the end of which beckon
God, wealth, sexual release – wags his finger. A warning.
It is his place, one lighter than most, the walls relieved of
        weight
The decorator gone mad
With assault-weapons.
Eat! Drink! Enjoy!
No more apologies.
God's hand in it.
        Magda, could that be?

    She's the sort who expects no love
And would only confuse it should you present the issue,
With a kind of getting by.
'See what you catch in a place like this?
Don't get smart with me or I'll punch your lights out.'
It's the proprietor laughing,
Ringfinger resting on his nose.
        Crucifix. Image of private parts exposed.

    It seems I was the one addressed,
Just a by-stander in this circus, Magda swinging on her trapeze.
She's the sort in a place like this
Who'd be ashamed if you saw her flinch,
        The game of chicken pointless.

Nahum and the Women of Ninevah

The women of Ninevah who were not spared
Had oiled their bodies and shone with pleasure.
    Their eyes reciprocated pleasure.
    Their bright toes were the image of pleasure.
It only reminded a prophet of his land.
    But so great was the delight his eyes swam in, he did not want
        the dream to end, Ninevah
The vision, men with chariots, with spears raised
    On the way to bring down her walls.
So that later, if you were to go and seek where the city
    had stood,
You'd seek in vain. What Ninevah?
Where were the happy girls, bright ribbons in their hair?
Then Nahum, he who knew, he who comforts, became even more
    pleased,
His dream now fact. And, as a prophet will, he published it,
    His compatriots taking heart from that.
And he looked out from the tower that gave him his view
    of the plain,
The horizon god-kissed,
And he measured more (because it is always being measured).
It is the most petty and sublime of measuring:
Who stays and who goes? It is as when the stars start tumbling
    end over end
And fair hope and politics drift
    Their inch across vast death-plains.

Oh, when the women of Ninevah had danced alluringly, when they
    shook themselves
And shivered pleasingly, and the soft, precious metals
That adorned them shimmered with sound,
It was as though warm winds suspired in gardens
    of love.
Yet, one may wonder what crimes they had fashioned,
    What oversights their gods were guilty of,
Whose ministrations were daily and so, not indifferent
    To each and every passion in its season.

Women help make light the life of banquets.
They mitigate the intense pursuit of blood sport
    As it is with young lions spending time beyond
      the high walls.
But such things did come to an end
And this mightily pleased Nahum,
And his eyes filled with what time the weapon
      Had counted out.

    Because now his enemies knew anguish.
The pride in them, the strength in them, the sheer joy in them
      of their viciousness
Was surpassed by the men from Babylon.
And they were a whirlwind of chariots, hearts saturated
    with purpose:
    They came and destroyed, –
Because vanity of mind is sovereign and power is casual
    As it ambles about in corridors
Building walls. And because life's rich, life gets along
    Without the mighty or the humble when they die,
When all have done with it at last
    And love the lovely places no longer. . . .

    The vision was deliverance to a man of Judah, of Elkosh.
Justice will have its just portions though it may seem
    to arrive
Too late. And in that city Babylon, supreme now after Ninevah,
    Judah's tribes would drown, would learn new vanities
      of the mind there.
And then it would come that there would be no more visions a
    prophet
Might publish, the god returned to what a god dreams,
    The sweet ground plowed under.
Some lonely, unspectacular dying was sinking its taproot.
    The god slept.
    Prophets ached.

    It is to be wondered, could Nahum – he who comforts –
Could he in the way one puts thumb and forefinger to a
    hard flame

And then pinches, could he tell if there
    The bony god, the lover on his rack,
    Was already housed, was in his pleasure?
Who was greediest for such cruelties as were needed
    To bring the world Shiloh?
Nahum, he who comforts, from his tower saw
The broad, human plain, how the godly feet were building
    darkness
On the hills. Nahum, he whose name means something
    like solace,
Saw all that, so much so it would seem that suffering
    might end,
And longing and satiation cease,
    History the dream
Or that in which dreams finish.

The November Propertius

Autumn went and friends fell away.
Those bastions of a sweet time are gone.
I made a list of who was left, and I counted less
          than a baker's dozen.
No more warm nights, puckish moons, guitars
          screaming at us
Inebriate on the lawns.
The meat was consumed and the wine was spilled,
The women made love to on elaborate tablecloths.
But the grail-weary horsemen are resting now
In the first flush of their isolations.
Everyone had been a rebel, everyone a head of state.
We are quite burned out of the business.
Some hour arrived.
I Propertius press
The roses in a book.

We forgot death had us beat, turning our heads,
Morning, noon, and night
With salutary thoughts of it.
As singers sang of love and health, in stature
          critics grew.
Not despair but false hope
Characterizes
Unease that drove us
Into each other's arms.

No more childless Wethersby, grand dame, contralto,
Regaling us in the meantime
With a tale of her husbands. The jealous sun – it had always
          strived
To pulverize the chintz she drew
Against the heat of the afternoon, against the pimps, whores and
          cops
Who were the starry spew of night.
And you, you on the phone, ring yourself off!
Think I care with what you slept?

As goodness was the rage, so meanness is the rule,
This pale November day fixed.

  In a funk like this, I'd drive to Scalinger's
        antique shop
In anticipation of cheer, in expectation of relief from
        being Propertius.
On the way I would admire the women in their frocks.
I would fiddle with the radio
And listen to light tunes
Of never-ending summer. Was it all directing me
Into the nearest stationary object?

  Edgar, pouting rose, he ought never have been born.
Prudent men shouldn't drink with louts.
    (That this was his line in certain loud places.)
The girls in black lipstick giggled. Girls thought him
        a soft and subtle relic.
The man spoke in pictures.
No one cracked the code:
. . . Chopin and liquor and horses
Steaming out on the snow, violet-eyed women dancing
        in hot rooms . . .
'Give it up,' I said to him.
Then I fell in love.

    – It was the thing, the gazing deep
Into each tender fright
Or the eyes that were Nel's.

  Scalinger sold vases and brass barometers, cigar-boxes, spoons,
        acanthus-topped pillars
From out of his shop, and the tourists bought these and
        other small deaths.
Scalinger, drunk, became moral. To tell you the truth, I couldn't
        abide the man:
The self-satisfied smile, the white hair, his head God's
        last silver bullet
Dreaming buffalo, dreaming foolishness at some
        Augustan court.

And Nel was tall and elegant the day she left me, and the day
        was casual, that day
In the airport lounge. The Fijian at the bar concocted,
With sweet, island eyes, mild sweet drinks
As the flights were called.
The jets taxied.
Such nonchalance!
I grew up in America, after all.
In the way a woman commands existence, bringing to
        the tasks of men
Weight and ease, my love conversed with me
From out of her disappointment.

'I am Propertius,' I shot back at her. 'I am no engineer.
I do not intend to be perfect in the eyes of you and the law.'
I figured I told the truth.
And we sat there among the travellers.
A girl was bound for Ottawa.
A young man would cruise El Salvador.
Cousin was off to seek cousin
In Yellowknife.

Nel, a queen, was fine among us.
Nel was headed for distant provinces.
Business! Family! Pleasure!
In the days of Croesus, oracles let one know
Life has sting: you win, you lose, it will rot.
A jagged nail of mine
Snagged Nel's nylon.
A plane roared by, throttle stupefyingly
Wide open. A miracle – the lift off.

Even so, power's the game, sex the court,
And then our deaths quiet us all. No more loved one, no more last laugh
        and penthouse
Though it was all you could have,
Nel at DEPARTURES.
I await my next captor. I expect
The usual bargain will be struck.

At loose in the wars of birth, I might have carved lions
      and bulls on palace gates
In a place – not L.A. – of palms and dates, brought
      Scalinger booty
And stole his daughter
Who was Nel. If one had to go and multiply, besides Fort Dix,
There was always the coming from out of Ur
In a dream of a new task, the galaxy swiftly moving,
Haberdashed in scarves of white and silk.

When I heard Nel was in Texas housekeeping, I would go see
Wethersby and complain, Edgar often there.
It was public what we slagged,
And it is a consortium
Of young darlings
Older than us. 'So let them die,' said Wethersby.
'Yes, rather,' agreed Edgar.
He'd done his bit.
And we stirred our tea
While the sun tore
Through Wethersby's protective chintz.
Nothing to be done.

Afterwards, that autumn spent, hairy Autumnus, his arm
      heavy
On me said, 'You'll get lonesome, the leaves falling,
Late blossoms dropping: mounting casualties.'
'You don't say,' I replied.
I was choking on his smell, his body putrid, his eyes
      crusted,
His hair wet and matted with verdure. . . . But who shall hide us
      from winter's face?
What's truth for men?
What will women believe?
I said that.
Autumn went.
Friends fell away.
I press the roses in a book.

In the Dead of Winter

In the dead of winter,
Wind deepening the chill,
I pushed through a door,
The patrons of the place
Anchored by newspapers.
The girl took my order.
The frothy, cream-pies looked
As though they'd sail off
Somewhere warmer, my elbows
    Propped on arborite.

The next thing I knew,
A man in from the street
Was beating his stiff body,
The ragged, over-stuffed
Coat rigid, his look ice.
But the fiver in his fist
Entitled him to stay,
So he settled down. He
Negotiated: the girl
    Would bring him toast.

On the TV, dance talk
And the demonstration:
A tango! and the woman
Snaked her elegance around
Her partner's smoothness,
And the severity – as he brought her low and bent to her –
Of limb to limb was style,
A picture of some
Endurance. I alone,
    It seemed, applauded.

No, no one there was impressed!
And the man consuming additives
Dug in his coat for a coin
That might soon prove his last

And spent the quarter.
This patriot unsung –
All things effortless
Treasonous, wasteful –
Introduced his parable:
　　He fed the jukebox.

　　Eventually, it was
Going to heat up. Snow
Would fall on the town
And headlights pierce gloom,
The cars losing motion,
The song gaining fast.
The rough voice-shiver of
The liturgy began
To underpin the age
With tone: its old
　　Acquisition of loss.

　　And that which lies beneath
Endeavour – lonely act –
Built its shaky world,
Raised its crown of death
On the virgin solace.
And anger and sadness
Competed for a corpse
In which desire rots.
'Too late, too late' I heard
　　From a standard blues measure.

　　The day nearly always
Wins, souls not easily
Seen or touched, though they
Are missed when they are lost,
The dancers educating.
Perhaps, it was all old hat to him –
The patriot sitting back,
Picking the plate clean
Of particles, his mouth a home
　　To satisfaction.

Me, I was recalling
A woman far from there
Who liked her music loud
And emotions intense,
Sex the image of them, –
Until men failed her and she,
Trying not to notice
Lack, made it more convenient.
Still, her gaze was too sharp
    For love's thin handout. . . .

A few flakes floating down
Now, thought and sense-impressions at one
With quickening snow . . . I read
Love is what saves, but it's
So much lonelier than that.
And the man with the coat,
Squalor-permeated coat,
Guffawed, rose, and left.
His time run out, he had
    Shot his bolt.

And she faded from my memory,
The vomit-caked blouse, the eyes
Wanting lullaby, her hands coarse
For all she wore soft garments
    And daintily directed mastery.

– Long after the café closes,
A bell ringing in the hush,
Pigeons huddled in pairs on roosts of stone,
    The world will have acquired honours,

Eternity a thing constructed of days
On which the hours are scratched
And of reaching like the blind
    Through the dark for more instruction.

On a Florida Beach

She glistens with lotion out next to the sea,
Eyelids trembling, the sky harsh with light.
The book did not hold her, old Europe the theme:
The prevailing against ruin and chance.
She had fussed with the chair
When I might not have bothered
    With the angle of recline.

★

She falls into sleep out by the sea.
All around, a crowd lies belly up or down.
Some read paperbacks, – some drink beer.
Others kick at the soft white sand.
Am I not jealous, I wonder?
The sun's her god, her pleasure.
And those men and those women
Celebrate their culture, –
And thoughts necessary to the unwinding
    Pattern their eyes.

★

She who is always restive before sleep comes,
An image of repose now, leaves unquiet to me.
I think a fear out of childhood returns
To join with what an adult fears.
In the way clouds pass over and briefly dull brightness
So memory's change and marauding sensation.
Perhaps that smell of salt on the breeze
Carries the scent of birth,
    And of the end, a glimmer.

★

Often in the evening when it's cool
We'll walk the beach, arms linked.
She'll sing to me, our strides matched
While the huge sun drops.
America is a wide land.
The going of the sun leaves us with nothing to say,
She so confident! but that our bodies are space,
   Qualities of love and ruin the vastness.

*

And she will dance on the beach to get me to smile.
She'll run and scatter birds.
Together they'll lift like a giant leaf,
Drift out and settle on the sea.
Then they'll fold their wings on the last shimmering light,
Then rise again in their thousands,
   Seemingly purposeful.

*

And we won't have been alone, so many others there
Holding hands, looking at the positive side of it all.
Then figures grow dark, voices distant.
Nightfall begins to dominate
The hotels and bungalows,
Lamps and televisions lighting windows.
The doom-habit's strong at this hour,
A so much smaller world now in focus,
   Folding its wings.

*

Her eyes fluttering open, she seems not to know where she is,
The beach busier.
Unsure what horizons are his to claim,
A boy kicks at a ball.
And what with the anxiety constricting his face,
I'll bet he believes he's failing!
   Everything's territory, isn't it?

Suddenly she sees him there and the fears he can't speak
And the troubles he can't explain, and the sun remains her
    pleasure.
She wriggles her toes, closes her eyes again.
Soon enough the boy will learn whom to punish,
Some old woman dragging him into the waves,
  His heart a wide room as terror pours in.

★

Old world, new world –
What's all that different?
Ruin prevails. Chance works
With small irritations and builds pearls.
But she sleeps, left alone. In her sleep she smiles,
  The sun, the wind, the soft white sand her heaven.

Parmenides living an exemplary life
        according to Eleatic wisdom
Mused that what changes
    Isn't true: what stays the same, what we imagine
        is real and permanent.
Almost October.
    A chill in the air.

Washing her windows before grime freezes to it,
The neighbour does not second-guess herself
    Out in the almost winter bare-armed,
        badly complexioned.

    And what with the moon that will rise tonight
        And run with chaos across the field, –
    What with her man drinking himself down
        While she camps on the couch and watches news,
    Some sky disappears from the sky above:
        Failure's cancelled on account of what's new.

Still, on this bit of earth she
And the likes of her and her man
    Crashing to the floor, and all of us, are lodged.

Hadrian's Villa

I went away. I arrived somewhere.
It was a rest I needed but, really, I had
No good reason to visit there.
Vague like this, I walked up the lane.
   The shade of the cypresses was pleasant.

   Time's permeable. I thought I might
Find the old heart at home
      in its tired house.
The shepherd in the field could have cared less.
   A woman nearby sketching away . . .
      a wind blowing leaves against her hair . . .

   I stood by the pool, the hazy sky
      unattached. I lit a cigarette, consoled
The stone Caryatides. Hot.
And the pine cones tumbled fatly
   Into time's own mirror.

   And the swans glided by.
And swallows chased swallows.
A cat licked its paw, –
   An old man whistled.

   Well, where had I been?
That I hadn't noticed him
Smug, self-sufficient,
   Arms spread along a bench!

   Even so, now it was clear: how we were ourselves
The remains of a small grandeur.
That tune he whistled 'The Happy Wanderer'.
He by his whistling's mocking tone
Was playful, confident. 'Hello,' he said
   To the spirit where it hid.

To M.K.

Steam tailing off the high roofs
    (some zero hour) bells ringing,
Snow falling
    In its absolute hush, –

Birds huddling on the ledges
As though they alone
Outlast what we dream
    Of paradise and holocausts –

Oh I tell myself,
'You live here.'

    And I lie about its comfort,
        And I lie about its beauty.

    And I lie even more about the importance
To knuckle down and say my duty,
Pimping for the muse again,
Pocketing the proceeds,
    Stringing her out.

    Not that on her own she can have come right
        The vagaries of existence.

    Poets will climb on pedestals
Knock themselves off,
Ears stuffed with noise,
Eyes dim, and now blind.
If I betray the dignity of art
To my appetites, I shall be the last to do so,
    For who gives a fig about either?

*

The night is infinite sexual promise,
    The city stretching out:

Its hubbub, its lights, and individual
   exploiting individual.

And the wind pulls harder on the trees below –
   To retrieve them.

To William Hoffer 1944-1997

Your leer corrected me, dismissed
What I said I knew of love
Back when we were old
Before our time, diseased with love.
You were unforgiving then, – I had not adored anyone
And would shut you out
If ever I learned to love.
'Where are the comrades,' you wrote to me,
Speaking of my poems.
'Where are their friends and what they love?'
And should the writer fail to tell a lover
Those parts of the sacrifice most choice
On which we in this unending winter would dine,
⠀⠀Then what's there to speak of?

⠀⠀Your hands were so careful: sometimes you held
⠀⠀⠀⠀⠀⠀a book in them
As though it were some
Exquisite flesh-eating flower.
And women said of you,
'Woman hater'. Men chimed in with much the same
Charge. And I, with perfect lack of charity, said
Women you had were easily had
⠀⠀And only with difficulty improved.

⠀⠀I said perhaps we had gotten proud.
You said the pride broken out in me
Was incurable. 'Enjoy your reward of failure,
You small like those other poets
Who have been making themselves large.'
This stung and then you died.
Let it serve the record: love formed the greatest
⠀⠀⠀⠀⠀⠀part
Of your being and your thought
For all its demanding
⠀⠀And strange passage through us.

Lines to the Memory of Roberta Yantis

An American highschool teacher,
Pious,
In deepest secrecy a maker of verse,
Kind, patient,
Favourite aunt to my sister's husband,
Liking cardplay and other amusements,
You are in your grave, the earth froze shut
   Though the sky is almost soft now, threatening snow.

*

Always a beginning seems to fall from grace
And the end's corrupt, and the kindnesses go
As no one, in the new life building,
Cares to remember what were
   Part and parcel of old cruelties.

And once gone they cannot be reconstructed.
If the kindnesses come at all they're stripped
Of their roots:
Love and hatred.
And maybe some dreamy
Laughter now
Threatens my insistence
That poetry's well-spring
   Is perverse.

In the way one recognized home by familiar landmarks,
By the land and the smells and the voices there enduring
From out of time to the end,
One might know what one had missed,
Now that one leaves behind betrayals one chose
And takes again a share of the old faiths, –
This 'how it was' a luxury too sweetly recapitulated,
   The pieties manufactured.

*

And you looked out a classroom window
At a landscape not yet suburban,
At a sky you would not instruct,
And your mind, that moment, was medieval
As when it was once believed
Light and number would give
Men nature's secrets, and love's house
Would stand on reason,
And Christ would pilot
The gravity-defying machine
Of the cross. You may have pondered:
What is it that runs sparrows,
That tells flowers 'Bloom'?
And a few exploratory words
As shy as boys and girls
Limb to limb at a first dance
    Came to be in you.

    But it was sometimes grim, how the American
Highschool teacher, alone in that room in her father's house,
Was retired,
Was by illness confined to a chair,
The angels departed, the gods wandered off
For one callous eternity
Of ultimate causation.
Then a muscle pushed her blood through veins,
The shadow on the violet papered wall her only friend,
The flies worshipped that had dropped from the air
And wrote her name on the window ledge
And the poet's soul
And the quality of love
    And extinction.

    And the solitary beds and the solitary truths
Of you and your heroes, of every mystic since
Your Christ
Are the dark things that were you, Miss Yantis.
I will let others argue the arguments
Of value. I do not wish you disremembered.
Smile on lines that follow I formed for you long ago

When I was all-knowing, amused, and tolerant –
My reward
For the lesson I was taught,
Good and evil caught out
    As useless superstitions.

*

May I presume and honour your memory
By an impulse as open to review
As a misdemeanour, a petty habit
    As most clandestine conduct?

How a bowl of sky sits over the valley
And cold mirrors the breath
And seems to brighten stars
    That carry the enclosure.

How a sky like this duns complaint
And diminishes gaudy dreams
Of any empire and any justice
    To the beauty of the heavens, –

And wisps of hair on brows like yours
And dust and gases and stray sparks
Familiar to the bottom crowds
    Further embellish the atmosphere.

The dead are dead. The living hope and fear
As it was when poems were real
As large acts, as brief epitaphs,
    And I was child enough to believe
        it was so.

You educated and you prayed, Miss Yantis, because you knew
Nothing else better to do,
Honest and unremarked by the better schooled, –
    Then you lived a private life, confined to a chair.

If those of your family who loved you let you lie,
Rude, it seems I will drag you through
The absolutes and the compromise
    In a present gathering speed,

    All the while there's the shiftless waiting,
The unreliability of connections between
American city, farm, and sky,
    Every moment of it, touting love and devotion, empty.

    But may this unwieldy structure repay you
Your refusal to shrink
        crabbed and small
    Though ultimates claimed the land.

The Apostle's Secretary

See how he glows – a Noah drunk,
The stars shining on the ruins of the ark.
See how he stares – Jerusalem's darling
Who came to write a gospel and a supplement.
From the first, I can't claim I ever got his drift.
Here in Ephesus evening draws close.
In Ephesus the beginning argues with the end.
Shouting in the street, a rabble feasts,
Loving gods that dance beyond his book.
And piled in the corner – those communiqués,
A month's worth left unread.
Tomorrow when he's rested,
With 'Greetings' and 'Amens',
He'll flatter the many supplicants
And the rich women in their houses
Will know themselves brave.
He needs this now: pride in the city,
Flowers and smoke smothering the street below,
The sailors on the arms of Sardis boys,
Or the measuring up of mountain girls, –
The chink of coins, the prate of a sage,
The hawker selling Love's figurines,
The executioner's rejoinder . . . This is his sphere
And all this he has just laid at the feet of a ghost.
This night, however, is as old as the earth:
Evening black on the boughs of trees,
Dread in the pit of the empty stomach.
Come, we will check the writing for mistakes
While that one out there – robbed – hollers, 'Thief!'
So stupid as to seek pleasure in the district.
We are all thieves here, and from this room,
The old man stole a god's agony.
So, peace be to thee, you now sleeping.

(Polycarp became the bishop of Smyrna, and is believed to have been a disciple of John and to have authored an epistle to the Philippians.)

I will leave the candle unlit.
But before I go to my own chamber,
As I hear love depart away from love –
Those voices out on the festive street
That the wind carries to the sea –
I'll soak the bread you left untouched
In the wine you didn't drink
And dream a terrible end.